DISCA

D0593673

ANSWERS FOR ALL OF LIFE'S QUESTIONS—

★ INSTANT ★

FORTUNE-
TELLER

★ AT YOUR FINGERTIPS! ★

ADAMS MEDIA

New York   London   Toronto   Sydney   New Delhi

▲adamsmedia

Adams Media
An Imprint of Simon & Schuster, Inc.
57 Littlefield Street
Avon, Massachusetts 02322

Copyright © 2019 by Simon & Schuster, Inc.

First Adams Media hardcover edition December 2019

ADAMS MEDIA and colophon are trademarks of Simon & Schuster.

For information about special discounts for bulk purchases, please contact Simon & Schuster Special Sales at 1-866-506-1949 or business@simonandschuster.com.

The Simon & Schuster Speakers Bureau can bring authors to your live event. For more information or to book an event contact the Simon & Schuster Speakers Bureau at 1-866-248-3049 or visit our website at www.simonspeakers.com.

Interior design by Michelle Kelly and Priscilla Yuen
Interior illustrations by Priscilla Yuen

Manufactured in the United States of America

10 9 8 7 6 5 4 3 2 1

Library of Congress Cataloging-in-Publication Data
Title: Instant fortune-teller / Adams Media (firm).
Description: Avon, Massachusetts: Adams Media, 2019.
Identifiers: LCCN 2019035662 | ISBN 9781507212165 (hc) | ISBN 9781507212172 (ebook)
Subjects: LCSH: Success--Quotations, maxims, etc. | Conduct of life--Quotations, maxims, etc. | Fortune-telling--Miscellanea.
Classification: LCC BJ1611.2 .I58 2019 | DDC 650.1--dc23
LC record available at https://lccn.loc.gov/2019035662

ISBN 978-1-5072-1216-5
ISBN 978-1-5072-1217-2 (ebook)

**Frustrated with your
tarot cards?**

◆◆◆

Sick of drinking tea?

◆◆◆

**Do you need your answer
from the universe NOW?**

The INSTANT FORTUNE-TELLER

is just what you need to tune into the energy
that the universe is sending your way in a snap,
simply by setting your intentions, closing your eyes,
and opening to the page that was divined just for you.
Check in whenever you need a little direction
in life, and get immediate answers about
the adventures (or misadventures)
coming your way.

You're right on the
edge of a breakthrough;
you just need to keep
pushing forward.

Don't let your bad day make someone else's worse. Be kind to those around you.

It might be scary, but you are ready to take some risks and explore new opportunities.

Your success is
100 percent guaranteed!
Go out and live
your best life.

Today is a great day to relax and do nothing. Celebrate this opportunity to disconnect!

It is the adversity you face that gives you the strength you need.

Your fortune is cloudy:
It looks like things are
up to you today.

You reap what you sow.
Sow joy and enjoy
your happiness harvest.
You're worth it!

You're building on something special. It will take some time to grow, but you've done the hard work; there's nothing left to do but sit back and wait.

Even a wrong turn
can put you on the
right path.

There's someone new in
your life whose presence
will be a gift for
years to come.

Life's presented you with a challenge. Relax and do the best you can!

Avoiding screens and immersing yourself in the now will ground you and provide much-needed perspective.

Keep an eye out for a problem with that big project you're working on. Everything might not be running as smoothly as it seems.

Your communication centers are running at full force today. Collaborate with someone on a new project, or take a friend out for lunch to chat.

You know you can do it,
but do you *want* to do it?
Make sure you're in touch
with what you really want
before you move forward.

Destiny is pulling you in a particular direction today; your best bet is to go along for the ride.

Get out of your comfort zone and explore new places. There's something exciting waiting for you!

Someone you count on may
have ulterior motives.
Proceed with caution!

Be careful! A financial
win doesn't mean you
should spend wildly.
Take a look at your
upcoming schedule and
plan accordingly.

You will have to overcome some roadblocks, but the reward you've been craving will be yours. Bide your time and work hard.

The thought of you
just brought a smile to
someone's face.

Don't trust everything
you hear today. Mixed
signals could lead to
some confusion and
unfair assumptions.

Do it. Do it now.
Do it now before you
regret not doing it!

Your decision to be healthier has already started to pay off. Keep up the good work!

A productive day
is ahead of you. You
will accomplish what
you set out to do.

Don't waste your energy
on regrets and self-doubt—
take a deep breath and
look forward to all your
future success.

Celebrate the
successes of people
close to you.

Don't sell yourself short!
You're a force of nature;
you just have to
believe in yourself.

You need a change of scenery. Try a new restaurant, choose a different route for your commute, explore a different part of your city—a little variety can go a long way.

Nothing is as bad as
it seems. Find the silver
lining and celebrate that.

Bad news is on its way.
Don't shoot the messenger
(in fact, consider thanking
them!), and do your
best to really listen.

You've got a great idea,
so speak up and share it!

Friends will be visiting
soon. Welcome them
with open arms and
open bottles.

Life is changing fast
for you. Accept it with
patience and good humor,
and good things
will blossom.

You've made a mistake.
You can choose to regret
it or to grow from it.

Luck is with you! Today is a
good day to take a chance,
try something new,
or ask for something
you really want.

You will feel the urge to overspend today: Make sure you think it through.

Take this as a learning opportunity, and you won't get schooled in the future.

A message of love is
coming to you soon:
Be on the lookout!

Your kindness and joy
have sparked interest
in someone you've
met recently.

★ ★ ★

Prepare for an extra boost of creativity. Be sure to give it lots of room to flourish!

A careless mistake could end up
causing more trouble than it's
worth today. Be sure to look
over all the details.

You've got all your ducks in a row and some extra money to spend. Splurge on a little something nice for yourself.

Hate to break it to you, but it might be healthier to start from scratch…

You need to look at where you keep ending up. If you want a change, you need to do something differently.

You have the ability to help someone in need today. Keep your eyes open and don't let the opportunity escape.

Enjoy the journey,
stumbles and all.

You've got a secret admirer!

Any guesses who?

Be on time today!
If you're late, you'll
end up missing out on
something special.

You're holding on to beliefs that don't fit who you are. You know you're ready to let them go.

Bad luck is in the air:
Be vigilant!

You've been
thinking about someone
from your past who still has
a role to play in your future.
Reach out and
reconnect.

The stars are aligned for cozy connections, so be open and friendly and see who you meet.

Just say yes! Let a positive
attitude lead the way.

Life doesn't always work out the way you plan. Roll with the changes and see where things take you.

A creative idea has sprouted. Be prepared to share with those who can help you make it bloom.

You're feeling a little lost today. Do something familiar to help yourself feel grounded.

Struggle is necessary for learning: Don't be afraid to push yourself a bit.

Positive energy is catching.

Spread yours around!

Distractions are making it hard for you to concentrate. Double-check all your work.

Wise people do not plot to get even. Your best option is to ignore the drama.

Trouble is looming on the horizon; act with care and kindness, and it will bypass you.

There's no such thing as knowing too much. Read up, and it will pay off.

You're feeling playful
and chatty today, and just
having fun. Take it easy,
and don't make any big
commitments.

Let your light shine.
Someone around you
needs to see it.

Proceed with caution.
Carelessness will hit you
twice as hard today.

You're in a good place to get things done, so roll up your sleeves.

There can only be one "worst day ever." Chances are it's not today.

Disappointment lurks.
Take it in stride—soon
the tide will turn.

Embrace the power of your body. Today is the perfect day to get up and move.

The winds of change are stirring, and you'll need to work hard to hold on to what you care about the most.

Don't force it:
If it's meant to be,
it will happen.

Something has been bothering you, and while it's important to stand up for what is right, it's also important to learn when to let go. Pick your battles carefully.

Think you're going in
the right direction?
Not so much...

Don't take it personally:
It's really not about you.

Pay attention to
your dreams this week:
They have something
to tell you.

Remember: You deserve
to be treated with love and
respect, *always.*

You are in a position
to be generous if you want to
be. Have some fun spreading
around what you have
in abundance!

Go outside for some fresh air and fresh perspective. It will help with the decision you've been mulling over.

Be spontaneous! It's a
good time to take a chance
and do something bold.

Sometimes you have to give something up to find what you've been looking for.

Stranger danger!
Not everyone is as they
seem today, so be on
your guard.

That thing you're waiting for...

it's on its way!

Confidence and hustle look
good on you: Work it!

Don't rush things. The path to success is marked by carefully planned steps.

Ask that question you've been afraid to ask.

Give yourself permission to be proud of everything you've been able to accomplish.

Sometimes it's a good thing to say no! Feel free to politely decline without an ounce of guilt.

Listen to your gut feeling to find the right path—it won't lead you astray.

Envy makes you blind to
the many good things you
already have.

There's a bitter taste in your mouth. Forgiveness can wash it out.

Feeling antsy? Look to your social network for your next project.

Your ideas will grow if you give them the space.

Put your trust in the universe, and it will get you where you need to go.

Someone has let the cat
out of the bag. Be careful
whom you trust.

Time to move on! Bigger
(and better!) things are
on the horizon for you.

You're feeling adventurous today. Spend some time planning a much-needed trip.

Watch your back.
Someone is eager to
steal your thunder.

Your hard work is paying off; now take this opportunity to *shine*!

You're feeling excited and joyful about a new opportunity—don't be afraid to share that enthusiasm with others.

Someone is thinking of you
with love right now—can
you feel it?

Switch around your routine
and shake things up a bit!

You can't move forward
when you're looking
behind you.

A new friend will bring
an exciting opportunity
into your life.

Your energy is heavy today. Wait until tomorrow for a fresh perspective before making a decision.

What you think you want

isn't good for your soul.

Put it aside and move along.

Reach out to those around you. Prioritizing career over connection will leave you lonely.

Sometimes all you need is a good night's sleep to replenish your mind, body, and spirit. Be sure to get one.

Take a moment to remind yourself that you are worth it. Don't let anyone make you feel like you aren't enough.

Unexpected changes are coming your way. Stay open-minded and see what new doors are opened.

You know what you want
and how to achieve it.

You're in for a big relationship shift. It's okay to get some space.

In a rut? Let your imagination run wild and your creative juices flow today.

A lucky day for new beginnings!
It's time to start something new
or renew a connection.

The abundance you
enjoy allows you the
freedom to be yourself.

When faced with a choice,
make it with confidence!
Your powers of reasoning
are at their peak.

Enjoy a little "me" time
today: You deserve it!

You are in for a period of
bad luck, but don't lose
heart: It is temporary.

Change can be painful,
but it often leads to a
better path.

Stop putting off that conversation you're dreading. You'll feel better when it's over and done with!

Relax. That stressful project will soon be over, and you can move on to better things.

Your worldview could use a new perspective. Be on the lookout for an opportunity to go somewhere you've never been before.

Being choosy is going
to lead you to the right
decision today.

Embrace mystery.
All will be revealed at
the right time.

You've hit an unexpected detour, but don't fear: You're still headed in the right direction.

Your talents will come into

play in a surprising way.

This isn't a good idea.
Stop, think, and come up
with a better option.

It's never too late to change
a bad habit. Start today
and don't look back.

Express gratitude today,
and it will be returned to
you many times over.

There are changes
you need to make to live
your best life. You know
what they are if you're
honest with yourself...

A pleasant surprise is

coming your way.

A chance you thought you missed will be coming back around. Keep your eyes open!

Don't frantically pursue peace, joy, and love. Let your heart be still, and these blessings will come to you on their own.

You are spending your time worrying about things that don't matter. Let go of your self-consciousness and live your life to the fullest.

Today is a good day
to make a change.

That thing you've been putting off? You can do it!

It's time for an adventure.
Pack a bag, hit the road,
and have yourself a real
experience.

Misery loves company,
so watch the company you keep.

Your home is filled to the brim with all the warm, fuzzy feelings: Get cozy and soak them in today.

You have a
new idea brewing—
it's a good one.

Connect with someone
new today. You'll be
glad you did.

Treat yourself. You know
you're worth it!

Keep your eyes on the prize and your foot on the gas. You've got this!

Your good intentions are
recognized. People see
your heart and love you
for what is in it.

Things have been busy
lately. Take some time to
slow your pace with a walk
down memory lane.

There's magic around today:

Keep an eye out for it.

You've reached a stalemate. It's time to try something different to get the ball rolling again.

You will soon
face a big challenge.
Approaching it head-on
will lead to the
best outcome.

Be careful with your words today. Something said with the best intentions could come off as harsh or deliberately cruel.

Think carefully and know
what's truly in your heart
before you act.

Today might not be
your day...but that's why
there's tomorrow.

A decision you've been waiting for will be decided in your favor.

Keep tabs on your bank account. You're going to take a financial hit soon from something unexpected.

Challenge yourself to try something new today. It will change your perspective and help you grow.

Celebrate your accomplishments. You are on your way to success!

Optimism and boundless energy fill your interactions today. Get out there and enjoy!

Today might be
a bit tough, so you may
need some extra energy.
Eat a good breakfast and be
prepared for a challenge.

Love is all around you.
All it takes is an open
heart to find it.

Your positivity attracts
good things to you.

Today, it is up to you
to create the happiness
you long for.

Someone special will enter your
life today; be open to
what is offered.

Cars (and people) can't
run on empty. Take a
moment to refuel.

Set aside time today to make progress toward an important goal.

Embrace your social
side and connect with
friends today for support
and comfort.

That delay today was meant to be. It put you on a course you're supposed to follow.

Guard your heart.
Trust is good, but
it should be earned.

Take a deep breath and
be patient. The solution
you're looking for will come
together in its own time.

You will get an unexpected
message today with
good news.

Change is always difficult,
so cut yourself some slack if
you have trouble adjusting.

You will have an addition
to the family by birth or
by choice, and your love
will multiply.

That new relationship
in your life? It has tons
of potential!

An unexpected
event will occur today that
challenges your beliefs.
Embrace it.

Sacrifice is hard. But a little pain now will bring you more joy and abundance in the future.

You will explore deep and
surprising topics in conversation
today. Don't shy away from
meaningful encounters.

The great outdoors is calling you today: Go out and greet it.

Watch out for energy vampires. Someone is trying to drain you of your good vibes; keep your distance.

Be gentle with
yourself today.

A much-needed rest is coming. Embrace it and receive new energy and direction for the future.

What you're looking for is within your reach! But you'll need to stretch a little.

Those around you are
noticing your hard work
and will acknowledge
your efforts today.

You're feeling stressed and concerned about the future. Talk out your concerns before making any major decisions.

Family—whether birth or chosen—is important. Reach out to someone you love and let them know.

Don't wait around for happiness to find you. Think about what you love and seek it out.

Your energy has been blocked for some time, but now it is flowing free. It's a good time to start something new.

Words have the power to hurt:
Be thoughtful about how you
speak to friends, strangers,
and yourself.

You've been denying it,
but you know something
needs to change.

A decision you made
in the past will come
back up. Stay strong in
your convictions.

You have a strong desire to
rekindle an old connection.
Follow your heart, and it
will lead you to love.

Sadness is a part of every life. Accept it, and let it remind you what is most important.

Things are going great,
thanks to you! Make sure
to take the credit.

Try again. You learned
something the first
time around.

You're headed toward a dead end. It's best to turn around and start again.

No matter what the
oracles say, you shape
your own future.

Too many nights on the couch with *Netflix* has you stuck: It's time to start something new and shake things up.

There's a secret in
the air, and it might
cause jealousy...

An unexpected change is going to throw off your plans; you can forge ahead, or take the new path that has opened up.

Enough suffering! It's time to make a clean break and move on.

You're up against new competition and will have to put in more of an effort.

You know the struggles you've overcome, so you know you're strong enough to stand up to the next challenge that comes along.

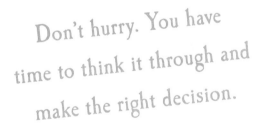

Don't hurry. You have
time to think it through and
make the right decision.

Things are happening!
Take a deep breath and
stick to the plan.

Mysterious forces are
at work to make things
happen for your benefit!

You're in for a slight delay,
but everything will work out.

Look to your mentor to help you plan your next steps. If you're thinking "I don't have a mentor," you need to look harder.

It can be hard to be
vulnerable and express
your real feelings,
but it's necessary.

Look for help from an
intuitive friend whose
judgment you trust.

You're out of balance: Nurture your softer side to reconnect to your lunar energy.

Today has
enough troubles of its own.
Don't borrow more from
the future by worrying
about things you
can't control.

Don't go along if you're not feeling it. You're strong enough to forge your own path.

That grudge you're still holding? The only one it's hurting is you. Let it go.

Today is a day
of abundance:
Go all out!

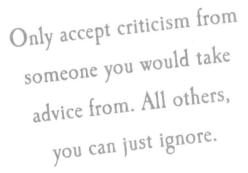

Only accept criticism from someone you would take advice from. All others, you can just ignore.

Stop being so indecisive. Go with your gut and make a choice. The only wrong decision is making no decision at all.

Sometimes things need
to end for something new
to begin. Embrace the
ending and look forward
to the beginning.

Caution: A new opportunity
may prove too good
to be true.